Contents

INFOTECH

Putting achievement first

INFO TeCH

Series Editor: Sue Hewer

5

Putting achievement first

Managing and leading ICT in the modern languages department

David Buckland

CiLT
Centre for Information
on Language Teaching and Research

The views expressed in this publication are the author's and do not necessarily represent those of CILT.

Acknowledgements
In order to illustrate the ideas in the book with concrete examples of activities, the author has consulted a variety of published and broadcast video courses.

Please note that, while information in the appendices is correct at the time of going to press, details may be subject to change.

First published in 2000 by the Centre for Information on Language Teaching and Research, 20 Bedfordbury, Covent Garden, London WC2N 4LB

Copyright © 2000 Centre for Information on Language Teaching and Research

ISBN 1 902031 63 6

2004 2003 2002 2001 2000 / 10 9 8 7 6 5 4 3 2 1

A catalogue record for this book is available from the British Library

Illustrations by Alex Buckland

Printed in Great Britain by Copyprint UK Ltd

CILT Publications are available from: **Central Books**, 99 Wallis Rd, London E9 5LN. Tel: 020 8986 4854. Fax: 020 8533 5821. Book trade representation (UK and Ireland): **Broadcast Book Services**, 2nd Floor, 248 Lavender Hill, London, SW11 1JL. Tel: 020 7924 5615. Fax: 020 7924 2165.

1 | Introduction

The reader

This book is for heads of modern foreign languages (MFLs) in schools, teachers of MFLs who have responsibility for managing Information and Communication Technology (ICT) in the department, teachers wishing to assume managerial responsibilities and teachers wishing to use ICT as a tool to support teaching and learning. It will also be a useful resource for ICT co-ordinators and school managers wishing to support the MFL department.

The aims

Its aims are to explain the importance of effective management if ICT is to raise achievement in MFLs and to provide guidance on how to manage effectively. In addition, it will identify sources of information and guidance that will help these aims to be met.

TERMINOLOGY

Before starting this book, it may be helpful to have a clear understanding of the following terms:

ICT (Information and Communications Technology)

(i) Computer-based hardware, software, information sources and associated technologies, e.g.

word-processors, databases, CD-ROM, the Internet, digital TV.

INFOTeCH
Putting achievement first

(ii) The knowledge, skills, understanding and values that pupils **need** to make effective use of the above tools, both in schools and in the outside world, e.g.

create presentations of good quality; make use of different information sources; show sensitivity to the feelings and needs of others.

In England and Wales, ICT is set out as a coherent body of curriculum content in the National Curriculum ICT Order. It is also a National Curriculum requirement for pupils to use ICT to support their learning in different subjects.

ICT capability

The knowledge, skills, understanding and values that pupils **acquire** through their use of ICT, both as a discrete subject and across the curriculum.

2

INFO TECH

Putting achievement first

2 Setting the scene

KEY PRINCIPLES

The contents of this book, the arguments it makes and the guidance it provides are based on four key principles. These are:

- The need to raise achievement.
- ICT can raise pupil achievement in MFLs.
- The use of ICT in MFL teaching and learning should always be appropriate.
- Pupils have an entitlement to use ICT to support and improve their language learning.

The need to raise achievement

The argument for the need to raise achievement in schools will not be repeated here. It has already been won at national level and is effectively reinforced by arrangements such as:

- the requirement to publish public examination results in school prospectuses;
- the publication, nationally and locally, of examination league tables;
- legislation requiring schools to publish their own achievement targets;
- inspection criteria requiring all aspects of a school to be judged in relation to the impact on 'the standards achieved by all of its pupils'.

School and departmental management systems, which in the past might have focused on managing staff, resources and the organisation, must now have a sharper purpose. Does this development plan, this in-service session, this meeting, this lesson plan, etc contribute **directly** to pupil attainment and progress? If not, what is it for? How can it be justified?

ICT can raise pupil achievement in MFLs

(i) by providing opportunities for pupils to:

*   communicate in the target language, e.g.
    through fax, e-mail, a word processor, presentation software;

*   develop and practise all four language skills, e.g.
    by using a multi-media CD-ROM to improve listening and pronunciation; by reading and summarising information found on the Internet; by drafting and redrafting work in a word processor;

*   enhance their language-learning skills, e.g.
    by using text manipulation software to develop written accuracy as well as knowledge of grammar and syntax;

*   develop or apply independent learning skills, e.g.
    by choosing appropriate practice activities within a tutorial program; by using appropriate strategies to search the Internet or to interrogate a database;

*   access resources in the target language, e.g.
    by accessing text, images and sound on the Internet or in a CD-ROM.

(ii) by helping pupils learn through experimentation:

The power to edit text and graphics, and to experiment with strategies for manipulating information, means that avoidance of mistakes needs no longer play a dominant role in teaching and learning. For example, a young writer wishing to write an account of a visit to Italy could first enter ideas and key vocabulary, at random and in note form. She could then organise and refine her ideas before finally expanding her notes into full sentences or paragraphs. At a later stage the work could be quickly and easily redrafted to improve both accuracy and range of language.

Once the activity has been completed, it will then be possible to discuss and reflect upon not only the finished piece of work but also the steps that were

4

taken to achieve it. *This will lead the learner to a clearer understanding of her own ways of learning which, in turn, will promote confidence, motivation and further achievement.*

(iii) by helping pupils work together through sharing and developing ideas:

The flexibility of thinking made possible by the use of ICT provides a natural platform for discussion and the sharing and developing of ideas. The position of the computer screen, which enables a small group to focus together on the work in hand, supports the collaborative process.

(iv) by helping pupils record, organise, investigate and interpret information:

The speed and power of ICT not only allows learners to do things quicker and more efficiently; it also enables them to do that which was previously impossible. For example, they could instantly access a German tourist information office on the world wide web, copy text and images from selected web pages into a word processor, amend the text, arrange the images and create an attractive and informative document.

5

As the quantity of information available increases, the ability to select, use and evaluate that information becomes increasingly important. Schools have a responsibility to help their pupils handle and structure information so as to be liberated rather than manipulated by it. This responsibility for teaching **about** *learning should be shared by all teachers.*

It is the task of management to ensure that the potential of these opportunities is realised.

That was fun!

The use of ICT in MFL teaching and learning should always be appropriate

- ICT is only **appropriate** when it enhances, supports and extends pupils' language learning in a way that could not be done with other methods or resources (the added value).

- Where ICT is **appropriate**, it should be used.

It's not acceptable to justify ICT use as merely enjoyable.

These are two powerful messages. They state that it is not acceptable to justify ICT use as merely 'motivating' or 'enjoyable' or 'a change'. They also imply that not only must departmental managers have a clear view of how ICT can raise achievement, they must then do everything possible to ensure that **appropriate** opportunities are provided – which leads to the final key principle ...

Pupils have an entitlement to use ICT to support and improve their language learning

6

Pupils learning a modern foreign language (MFL) have an entitlement to use IT:
- to communicate in the target language;
- to communicate with people of the target languages and communities;
- to develop and improve all four language skills;
- to enhance their language-learning skills, e.g. to develop their understanding of underlying structures;
- to develop or enhance independent learning skills;
- to access a range of resources in the target language and identify with the people of target language communities and countries;
- to meet their special needs for access to language learning;
- to make effective use of and extend existing IT capability.

Language teachers have an entitlement to the training and resources they need to enable them to implement their pupils' entitlement.

Extracts from *MFL: an entitlement to IT* – available free from BECTA

This is an entitlement for **all** pupils:

- irrespective of ability
  ICT use should not just be available for the least or most able pupils;

- irrespective of the teacher
  if only one or two classes in a year group are using ICT appropriately, entitlement is not being met.

INFO**T**e**CH**
Putting achievement first

A key task of management is to plan for this entitlement, to ensure that it is in place and to have a clear picture of the intended improvements in pupil learning.

You will find details about pupil and teacher entitlement at: vtc.ngfl.gov.uk/resource/cits/mfl/ictandmfl/index.html

KEY CONTEXTS

In applying principles, it is vital to take into account the context within which this will happen. The principles set out above will need to be applied in schools in contexts where:

Departments are increasingly accountable for their performance

For example, they are expected to:

- have a clear picture of their pupils' progress in order to set appropriate targets and make the changes necessary to ensure the targets will be met;

- produce development plans in which the correct priorities are identified and the action taken is effective;

- ensure that time and money spent on training leads directly to improvement in pupil achievement;

- ensure equality of opportunity; if some pupils enjoy a better curriculum provision than others, carry out more productive activities and use a greater range of appropriate resources, this means that equality of opportunity is lacking.

Opportunities and expectations concerning the use of ICT in schools are increasing

For example:

- the revised National Curriculum Order for MFLs now contains explicit references to the use of ICT in its Programme of Study, e.g. use of material from the Internet when teaching about different countries and cultures;

7

INFOTECH
Putting achievement first

- newly qualified teachers, when assessed, must now demonstrate the ability to select and make good use of ICT resources which enable teaching objectives to be met;

- the National Grid for Learning (NGfL) is using the power and availability of the Internet to provide a wide range of teaching and learning opportunities;

- the teacher training programme established under the NGfL initiative and financed by the New Opportunities Fund (NOF) will ensure that all teachers gain at least the level of competence and confidence now expected of all new entrants to the profession.

These contexts will undoubtedly support and strengthen MFL teachers and managers wishing to make effective use of ICT. Equally, these new developments could be threatening to departments that until now have been unwilling to take ICT seriously. It isn't going to go away!

8 ICT IN SCHOOLS

Despite the encouraging developments taking place at national level, the fact remains that even for the most committed, organised and imaginative departments, the school environment poses a range of problems. These include:

- the crisis of MFL teacher recruitment and retention;

- demands on teachers' time and energy that have little to do with raising achievement;

- a lack of reliable information, based on credible research, about how and what pupils learn best when using ICT – this does little to diminish the scepticism of colleagues who have lived through other false dawns such as the language lab and the 'audio-visual approach';

- the need to depend on people outside the department (e.g. the ICT co-ordinator) in order to bring about change;

- the increasing pace of technology and the need for schools to adapt to these changes (why can't everything stop for five years so that I can catch up!);

- the lack of control and authority that some teachers may experience (for example, when confronted by computer whizz-kids in Year 7);

INFO TECH
Putting achievement first

- under-resourcing (always an issue until each pupil has access to a computer whenever and wherever one is needed!);

- difficulties in accessing central school resources, e.g. computer rooms;

- lack of technical knowledge (it's all right until the machine does something I don't understand!);

- insufficient ancillary / technical support.

These difficulties will always be present to a greater or lesser extent in all departments.

THE CASE FOR LEADERSHIP AND MANAGEMENT

It is easy to see that without good management the day-to-day challenges presented by the school environment will result in, at best, patchy, inconsistent and ineffective ICT provision, to the detriment of learning.

On a more positive note, there is evidence that the success of MFL departments which currently ensure effective teaching and learning with ICT is not necessarily due to exceptional resources or stability of staffing. These departments are characterised by:

- having a clear and unambiguous purpose for the use of ICT, i.e. to support learning and raise achievement;

- using a limited number of ICT applications consistently and effectively with whole year groups;

- including ICT activities in schemes of work so that all teachers are required to teach them;

- having in place systems for monitoring and evaluating the effectiveness of ICT in terms of learning outcomes;

- being able to undergo change successfully and without stress.

To achieve this, these departments have been supported by good leaders and managers.

9

INFOTECH
Putting achievement first

Management and leadership are often used as synonyms. Broadly speaking, however, they may be distinguished as shown below. A department may be well managed but poorly led. The opposite is also possible.

Good managers

Good managers are concerned largely with the successful execution of identified tasks and responsibilities.

They successfully deploy available resources (human, physical and financial) to meet the objectives of the department.

This helps to promote efficiency (i.e. making the teacher's job effective, manageable, achievable and sustainable) which in turn leads to good working relationships.

Good leaders

10

Good leaders are concerned above all with directing the department's efforts towards attainment, rather than other issues.

They know that the main factor in raising achievement will be good teaching. They therefore do everything possible to ensure that there is a clear direction to the way in which teaching and learning resources are used.

They monitor the work of both teachers and pupils. Underachievement is challenged.

They are directly involved in classroom improvement and are able to give direct, practical advice about how to raise attainment.

They develop an ethos for the department in which pupils and teachers value their achievements, try hard and encourage others.

It should be noted that staff without management responsibilities can exercise a leadership role. For example, both enthusiastic and negative colleagues can affect the way in which change is pursued.

The head of department may not automatically assume both leadership and management roles with regard to ICT. For example, in many departments younger colleagues have been given this responsibility. When this occurs, however, it remains the responsibility of the head of department to:

- provide a clear job description, with a focus on raising achievement as well as on administrative tasks;

- work alongside the colleague to reach a shared 'vision' of ICT for the department (i.e. a clear view of successful practice at lesson level, and how it can be achieved);

- ensure that the colleague's vision is understood, shared and implemented by the whole department;

- support and consult, as appropriate.

With the above points in mind, some departments may consider sharing the responsibility for ICT development between a good leader and a good manager. If this is to occur, good communication will be essential; otherwise managers will not be clear about what they are managing and leaders will lack the means to bring about change.

In the next chapter practical guidance is provided to enable departments to formalise their ICT policy and to further ICT development in the service of language teaching and learning.

11

INFOTeCH
Putting achievement first

3 Knowing where you are – the departmental ICT policy

For ICT to be successfully integrated into teaching and learning, subject departments need policies which set out a basis for the management of such issues as resourcing, access, staff development and use in the curriculum.

However, before providing guidance on what the ICT policy should contain, it will be important to establish a clear view of:

- its purpose;
- its format;
- its audience;
- the contexts that it must reflect.

It will then be possible to set out some recommendations for:

- the policy's content;
- how to make it work;
- how to check if it is working.

PURPOSE

As with all departmental documentation, the ICT policy must be a working tool to help the department do its job efficiently and consistently.

The policy will be a **management tool**; for example, it will identify responsibilities and support the effective deployment of resources.

It will also be a **leadership tool**, since it will emphasise the purpose of ICT in the teaching and learning of MFLs. This will ensure that the department's efforts remain focused on the attainment of all pupils.

Of course there is little point in having policy documents if they are not followed. The ICT policy should therefore have status. Indeed, it could be argued that written policies for ICT, at both school and departmental levels, are part of the general legal requirement upon governing bodies to produce policy statements. Where necessary, the policy should also require compliance.

FORMAT

Essentially, any format will do, although some departments may be constrained by specific whole-school guidelines as regards format, headings etc.

·The policy should be in a location where it is readily accessible to the whole department.

A master version of the main text on disc is essential.

AUDIENCE

13

The policy will need to be understood by many audiences, e.g. departmental colleagues, senior managers, staff in other departments, governors, parents, advisers, inspectors, commercial sponsors.

This means that although it is primarily a working tool for the department, abbreviations and specialist terms will need to be avoided or explained.

CONTEXTS

To understand fully the department's ICT policy, its audience will need to be aware of two key contexts that will influence its content and approach. These are:

■ National Curriculum requirements.
■ The school's approach to delivering ICT capability.

National Curriculum requirements (for teachers in England and Wales)

Background

ICT has a unique position in the curriculum. On the one hand, it is a National Curriculum subject in its own right, with its own programmes of study and attainment targets. On the other hand, it is a resource for teaching and learning which must be developed and applied in all subjects because:

- it can enhance teaching and learning by providing a unique and powerful way for pupils to record, organise, investigate and interpret information;

- it can develop the individual's overall ICT capability by providing a rich source of contexts for applying newly acquired knowledge, skills and understanding.

This view is supported by the OFSTED framework which requires the inspection of ICT to draw on evidence from all subjects inspected.

14

The current position

The requirements for ICT use in the MFL programme of study (from September 2000) include:

- skimming and scanning written texts for information;
- working with authentic materials in the target language;
- producing and responding to different types of spoken or written language;
- accessing and communicating information;
- redrafting writing to improve its accuracy and presentation.

Key points

The following points may be useful in enabling teachers to develop and operate a coherent and sensible policy that will help them to meet subject requirements, making best use of their current assets:

- ICT can support language learning:

  - when pupils use knowledge, skills and understanding that may be relevant to a range of curriculum areas, e.g.
    they create and edit text in a word processor when drafting and redrafting; they use a search engine to find information on the Internet;

INFOTECH
Putting achievement first

- when pupils learn and apply specific aspects of ICT that are unique to the subject, e.g.
  they use a target language spell-checker to check, reflect on, analyse and improve their work; they use text manipulation software to develop grammatical understanding.

■ Use of ICT is 'appropriate' when it is more effective than other resources in achieving a specific language-learning objective.

■ When appropriate, ICT should be used.

■ Pupil entitlement is only met when all pupils in a whole year group are given similar opportunities to develop their language knowledge, skills and understanding through the use of ICT.

■ The priority of ensuring entitlement does not preclude other work from going on in order to:

- meet the specific needs of individual pupils or groups, e.g.
  find information from the Internet for a GCSE oral presentation, support a pupil with writing difficulties;

- carry out a pilot project with a single class prior to dissemination and expansion at a later stage, e.g.
  work with a class using text manipulation software to model GCSE essays at grades C and A.

■ All teachers must have a clear understanding of MFL National Curriculum requirements concerning the use of ICT.

■ Departments must show that they are satisfying these requirements as far as their current capabilities and resources allow. Progress should become increasingly secure:

- as national targets for teacher training in ICT are met;

- as schools develop more flexible and imaginative approaches to the use of resources both in timetabled lessons and elsewhere (e.g. the learning resource area/library, the home).

15

INFOTECH

Putting achievement first

The school's approach to delivering ICT capability

Background

The content and implementation of the department's policy will be influenced by the school's approach to the delivery of ICT capability. This will normally reflect one of the following models:

(i) The ICT programme of study is delivered to all pupils centrally through a clearly defined programme. ICT may also be used in subject areas, but this is not mapped or co-ordinated.

(ii) There is a small central core of ICT running through each year aimed at developing skills which can then be used across the curriculum. Subject departments are expected to identify areas of their curriculum where these skills can be applied and reinforced. It may be possible for some aspects of pupils' ICT capability to be assessed through their work in subjects.

16

(iii) Central ICT skills training only takes place at the beginning of Key Stage 3. All further development is through cross-curricular use, with a small number of departments taking a leading role in both delivery and assessment.

(iv) Delivery of ICT capability is entirely cross-curricular, with departments agreeing which components they will teach and assess. This approach requires high degrees of staff competence and curriculum management in order to ensure both coverage and pupil progression.

The current position

Model (i) is the most common. It has the advantage of being the most straightforward to implement, requiring no cross-curricular planning, tracking, monitoring and assessing. It also guarantees a similar core experience for all pupils. This guarantee of consistency is likely to be less secure when ICT is devolved to departments where skills and experience may be diverse (owing to inconsistent training provision nationally) and unstable (owing to staff mobility).

However, this centralised approach also has potential disadvantages, namely:

■ pupils' prior experience (which will be varied) may not be sufficiently recognised;

- the contexts in which ICT skills are taught may lack breadth, relevance and variety;

- an *ad hoc* approach to delivery in subject areas deprives pupils of planned opportunities to apply their skills in new contexts.

These disadvantages have to some extent been addressed by the model scheme of work supporting the ICT component of the revised National Curriculum. This detailed (non-statutory) scheme of work provides both relevant contexts and opportunities for differentiation. It should sit comfortably with the ICT subject requirements since it can:

- provide all pupils with a foundation of knowledge, skills and understanding (as in current literacy and numeracy programmes) that can then be transferred to the curriculum;

- free subject teachers from the need to spend time on the teaching and assessment of ICT skills.

The reality in schools, however, is not usually as clear cut as the above descriptions might imply. For example:

17

- The delivery of ICT capability in many schools will not correspond exactly to one of the above models. There is a wide spectrum of approaches across the secondary sector.

- In schools following a centralised approach, work in departments may be delayed because essential skills have not yet been taught in the core programme. For this to be avoided either the school will have to modify its programme, or the department will have to take on the responsibility of teaching the skills needed.

- A school successfully delivering ICT across the curriculum may need to revise its approach following the departure of key staff whose replacements are less ICT-competent and experienced.

Key points

The following points may be useful in helping teachers develop and operate a policy that best supports their own teaching whilst fitting in with the school's chosen approach to delivering ICT as a National Curriculum subject:

- Delivering ICT capability as an ICT requirement is different from consolidating and developing ICT capability as a subject requirement.

- A department only delivers ICT capability if it actively plans to move pupils on from their current level of competence in ICT.

- If this is to happen, teachers will need to know about the progression in ICT skills and capability as set out in the National Curriculum orders. They will also need resources, time and training. Most important, they will need to be satisfied that any proposed work is appropriate. The tail must not be allowed to wag the dog!

- If teachers of MFLs are expected to assess pupils' ICT capability, they must be competent and confident to do so. This will require training – not necessarily a priority with most MFL teachers, who may feel that their time is better spent elsewhere.

- Whatever the school's approach, the department must know exactly what it is expected (and not expected) to do.

- To assist planning, departments need to know, at any time, what skills their pupils possess as a result of their work in a centralised ICT programme or in other subject areas. It is the school's responsibility to make this information readily available to all staff.

- Departments in turn must be responsible for informing the ICT co-ordinator of their own work (both planned and current), so that this information can be passed on to others. Clearly, the more the ICT co-ordinator knows about the work taking place in the department, the more (s)he will be able to help. Communication is a two way process!

18

CONTENT

Many policies gather dust in filing cabinets because:

- they contain too much philosophical discussion about, for example, the advantages of using ICT;

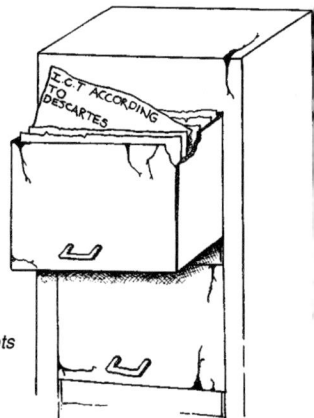

Many policies gather dust in filing cabinets

INFO**T**e**CH**

Putting achievement first

- they are not of practical use to teachers in their day-to-day work.

This has been born in mind when offering the following suggestions for the content of a departmental policy. The advice is not to go overboard. Much can be agreed or found out quickly, written up briefly and then, if necessary, expanded over time. Some suggested content may already exist elsewhere, e.g. with the school's ICT co-ordinator or in the school's main ICT policy document.

Stating beliefs and intentions

A rationale for teaching and learning using ICT

Keep this brief, accentuating the value-added. For a more detailed rationale of specific applications, e.g. text manipulation, word processing, data handling, e-mail, the World Wide Web, you may wish to refer to the National Grid for Learning's 'MFLIT' website as well as books and documents available in the department.

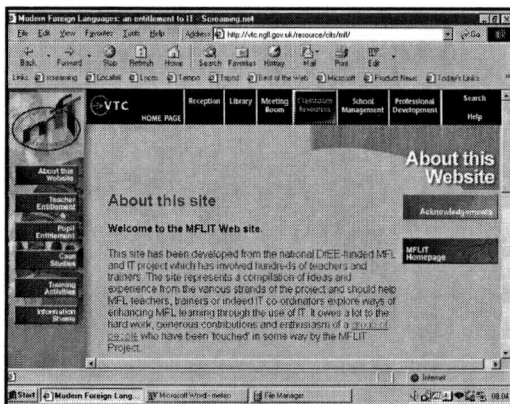

You may wish to refer to the MFLIT website

Pupil entitlement

Again, keep it brief and clear. You may wish to refer to points made elsewhere in this book and to the MFL and ICT Entitlement document available from BECTA.

19

INFO TECH

Putting achievement first

Describing the current position

ICT in teaching and learning

Briefly refer to all instances where pupil entitlement is being met and where use of ICT is a requirement of all staff, e.g. in Year 8, use of text manipulation software to model what a good piece of writing might look like. This should be described in greater detail in the scheme of work.

Also refer to other work taking place with individual teachers, classes or groups of pupils. This should be described in greater detail in the ICT development plan.

The school's approach to delivering ICT capability

Should be set out in the whole-school policy.

The department's contribution (if any) to ICT capability

Such as the teaching of e-mail skills within the context of a class link.

Staff competence and experience

Such as basic disc and file management, combining text and pictures in a word processor, creating files in a text manipulation package, copying text from the Internet into a word processor, interrogating a named database, drafting and redrafting.

Resources – hardware

What does the department own? Where, and on what conditions, does it have access to other resources, e.g. computer rooms, the LRC (learning resource centre/library)? What proportion of pupils have access at home to a word processor/the Internet?

Resources – software

Which generic software (e.g. Microsoft Word) is owned centrally and used throughout the school? Which software is MFL specific? Is all software to be found on all accessible computers?

Resources – systems and procedures

Such as logging on and off the network, using printers, booking into a computer room or the LRC, reporting faults and problems, permitted use of floppy discs, checking for viruses.

20

INFO TECH
Putting achievement first

Roles and responsibilities

What are the responsibilities of the HoD/all teachers in the department? Is there a departmental ICT co-ordinator? Does (s)he have a job description? How does (s)he liaise with the HoD, colleagues responsible for schemes of work and development planning, the school's ICT co-ordinator, other curriculum areas? Does the school differentiate between the roles of ICT co-ordinator (curriculum) and computer/network manager (technical)?

Channels of communication

Is there a school ICT management group? If so, is the department represented? If not, how is its voice heard? Are there any formal links between the department and the school's ICT co-ordinator? Who makes decisions concerning access to resources? On what basis are these decisions made? Does the department set aside time (e.g. in departmental meetings) to plan and review its use of ICT?

Staff development opportunities

How are needs identified? Are opportunities open to all? What opportunities are available:

- within the department?
- within the school?
- within the LEA?
- from outside providers?
- from national programmes?

How is staff development evaluated?

Technical support

Who provides this support? How do you go about requesting it? What level of technical expertise is available within the department?

21

MAKING IT WORK

Policies exist on two levels, i.e.

- what is actually happening;
- what is on paper.

INFOT℮CH
Putting achievement first

The most effective policies will, of course, be those in which paper and action are most closely matched. For this to happen:

The department will have to believe that ICT can raise achievement

This should not be taken for granted. A typical department is likely to contain teachers who are sceptical about the worth of ICT because they:

- lack the capability they need to teach the pupils;
- lack confidence;
- have had bad experiences of using ICT due to technical problems, classroom management difficulties or lack of impact on pupil achievement.

The only way to address this problem is to welcome feedback and comment when the ICT policy is being created or reviewed. Misgivings must be aired and experiences must be shared.

It is then the task of the HoD (and/or the department's ICT representative) to:

- provide real examples of successful and achievable learning outcomes emerging from ICT use with pupils, if possible from within the school rather than from documented case studies (although it would be helpful to have these available for reference);

- note down misgivings that can be attributed to leadership and management deficiencies, e.g. lack of clear learning objectives when using ICT; need for guidance and training in both software and classroom management; insufficient technical support; poor communication;

- ensure that these misgivings are systematically addressed within a policy implementation plan; otherwise, all future development work will be insecure and the aim of pupil entitlement will be compromised.

The department will have to own the policy

Ownership does not mean that the policy must be written collaboratively. However, it must be presented to the full department for discussion and amendment (when being created) or for annual review. Successful implementation is more likely if staff views have been sought than if the policy has been imposed without consultation.

22

A printed copy of the policy should be readily available at all times. Since the policy is a working document, colleagues should be encouraged to make comments or contributions at any time, perhaps by writing in pencil or by using 'post-it' notes.

CHECKING THAT IT'S WORKING

To judge whether the policy is providing appropriate information and guidance, the department could anticipate a number of practical situations in which reference to the policy may be needed, e.g.

- the school's ICT co-ordinator wants to find out whether any pupils in Year 9 are using the Internet or databases in their MFL lessons;
- a teacher being interviewed for a vacant post asks whether she will be required to deliver ICT capability in her lessons;
- a new teacher taking over a Year 10 class wants to know how the class can get access to the Internet in order to find examples of French pupils writing descriptions of themselves;

23

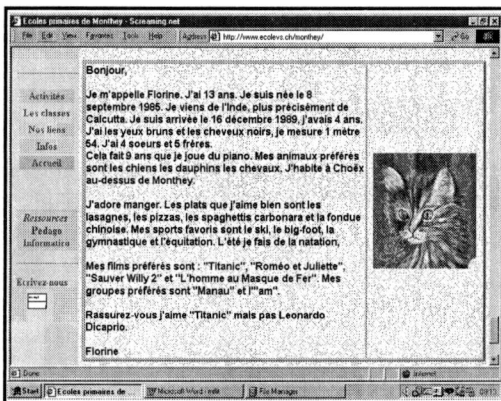

Useful texts ... but can the classes get access?

- an inspector is checking whether ICT opportunities are made available to all pupils in Year 8;
- the head of English wants to find examples of successful ICT use in MFLs;

INFO TeCH

Putting achievement first

- the senior teacher in charge of INSET wants to know if the department needs more training in order to make adequate use of its own ICT resources.

If all members of the department are able to respond to these anticipated situations in a consistent and confident way, it will mean that the content of the policy is appropriate and that it has been understood.

Better still, members of the department could be asked to recall real situations that have arisen, e.g.

- a teacher needed to know if a text manipulation program was available on the computers in the LRC;
- a teacher needed to know how to book a class into a computer room;
- the senior teacher in charge of resources needed to find out if the department was making adequate use of its own ICT resources;
- a teacher needed to know how to find out whether all pupils in her Year 9 class had prior experience of using a specific data handling program;
- a parent wanted to know if it was acceptable for her son to produce his homework on a word processor;
- a teacher wanted to know if anyone in the department was able to teach her how to create tables in a word processor;
- a governor was investigating whether the department had sufficient access to resources to meet its needs.

They could then discuss how these situations were dealt with.

If they were able to respond in a manner consistent with the policy, it will mean that the content of the policy is appropriate and that staff are able to apply their understanding, thus confirming that the policy is a useful and practical working document.

If this is not the case, there will be a need to either review the policy's contents or to ensure that the policy is accessible and understood.

In conclusion, it should be apparent that a practical and coherent ICT policy will give the department's management team a secure foundation for the vital task of planning for achievement. This is dealt with in the next chapter.

24

4 Planning for action

Planning for ICT needs to feature within the departmental development plan which sets targets and explains how they are to be met.

It should also figure within the departmental scheme of work which sets out guidance for teaching so that provision can be sustained consistently across classes and over time.

THE DEVELOPMENT PLAN

The cycle of development planning is now well established in schools, but, in practice, the planning process can have shortcomings. This happens when plans are more about tasks than outcomes.

For example, they refer to broad focus areas such as differentiation, writing, target language, ICT, and list things that teachers will do in these areas, e.g. attend courses, write documentation, order new text books, provide opportunities for pupils to do things.

However, they tend to say little about how pupil performance will improve as a result of these tasks being done.

Setting concrete intentions

These shortcomings can be avoided by ensuring that all development planning is based on concrete intentions that:

- are clear, detailed and explicit;
- focus on pupil achievement;
- give a clear purpose to the tasks that will need to be done.

INFO TECH
Putting achievement first

Here are two examples of what this might look like.

Example 1

A starting point such as ...

Pupils need to do more independent reading.

... could be developed into the following concrete intentions:

Each term at least three lessons and three homeworks will be set aside for Year 10 pupils to read, on an individual basis, texts from different sources, including:

* *readers;*
* *newspapers and magazines;*
* *the Internet.*

Teaching to support this work will include showing pupils how to:

* *use context, cognates and grammatical clues to interpret meaning;*
* *make appropriate choices from a range of texts;*
* *use a dictionary effectively.*

Pupils will respond to texts in different ways, e.g. discuss, summarise, find details quickly, extract items for a written or spoken task.

Their progress will be seen in terms of:

* *reading with greater confidence and enjoyment;*
* *tackling more demanding texts;*
* *extracting a greater depth of meaning;*
* *an improvement in performance at GCSE.*

26

Info Tech

Putting achievement first

Example 2

A starting point such as …

We need to identify ways in which pupils might make good use of ICT in Year 8.

… could be developed into the following concrete intentions:

All Year 8 pupils will use the Fun With Texts *text manipulation program to work with models of writing reflecting National Curriculum levels 3, 4 and 5.*

This will take place in at least three different contexts during the year.

Preparation will involve familiarising pupils with:

* *the vocabulary of the model and its pronunciation;*
* *key aspects of grammar demonstrated in the model.*

Work at the computer will normally follow the sequence of:

* *Copywrite easy (read the text for as long as you like);*
* *Prediction;*
* *Clozewrite.*

Follow-up work will show pupils how to emulate the models by:

* *substituting words and phrases;*
* *using aids such as exercise books and text books, dictionaries and glossaries;*
* *acquiring techniques for memorisation.*

Their progress will be seen in terms of:

* *working at the computer with greater independence and speed;*
* *working productively at the computer with a partner;*
* *writing more accurately;*
* *being able to make substitutions to a model in order to write their own accounts;*
* *writing longer passages from memory;*
* *an improvement in performance in AT4 at the end of the year and at the end of Key Stage 3.*

27

INFO**T**e**CH**
Putting achievement first

Starting points

It should be noted that Example 1 includes the use of ICT as part of an overall plan to improve reading, whereas Example 2 is based specifically on using ICT.

Both examples, however, emphasise concrete intentions for pupil learning, supported by criteria for judging whether learning has taken place.

Leadership

Deciding when and how to include ICT in departmental development planning requires leadership qualities that:

- direct the use of ICT towards attainment in the foreign language;

- make appropriate choices of ICT applications, in terms of both their effectiveness and manageability;

- convince colleagues that these choices are appropriate – through explanation, reference to documented case studies or, best of all, evidence drawn from pilot work that has already taken place in the department.

Tasks

Once intentions have been established, the development plan can then identify the tasks (with timescales) needed to bring them to fruition.

Key tasks related to ICT within the development planning cycle are:

Timing the work

This could involve pupils using computers:

- *regularly (say once a week) over an extended period of time;*
or
- *in a concentrated block of lessons.*

Planning the work across a year group, to ensure that entitlement for all is met

This could involve:

- *the whole year group using ICT over the same period of time, e.g. within a unit of work planned for February and March;*

28

INFO TECH

Putting achievement first

or

- *different classes making similar use of ICT, but at different times, e.g. class A uses a word processor to draft and redraft text in October, whereas class B does this in November.*

Ensuring that access to computers will be possible

This is likely to involve negotiation with the ICT co-ordinator.

It may also need some imaginative approaches to providing alternative forms of access when a computer room is not automatically available.

Examples of alternative arrangements for the Internet could be:

- *Year 10 access to a computer room is agreed for June and July when the room is no longer needed by Year 11 and 13 computer studies classes.*

- *An MFL department with a single computer connected to the Internet is planning, over the course of the year, for each Year 9 pupil to find websites containing information to support the current topic.*

  Arrangements are made for the computer to be available at times when low-level staff supervision is possible, e.g. during lunch breaks and on two days after school.

  Each week, three pairs of pupils are given access to the computer, so that over the year the issue of entitlement for all 200 pupils in the year is resolved.

  Pressure on access to the single computer is eased when a number of pupils decide not to do the work in school because they have the Internet at home.

- *Pupils in Year 8 are required to gather specific information from a bank of pre-selected websites in order to support work taking place in the contexts of food (term 1), leisure (term 2) and animals (term 3).*

  To make this possible, they are given priority access to four of the computers in the learning resources area before school, during the lunch break and after school.

  Alternatively, they can do their work at home if they have Internet access.

  The manager of the learning resources area agrees to keep a record of work completed. Teachers of the Year 8 classes monitor these records and get feedback from their pupils about learning, enjoyment and any problems encountered.

29

Planning for action

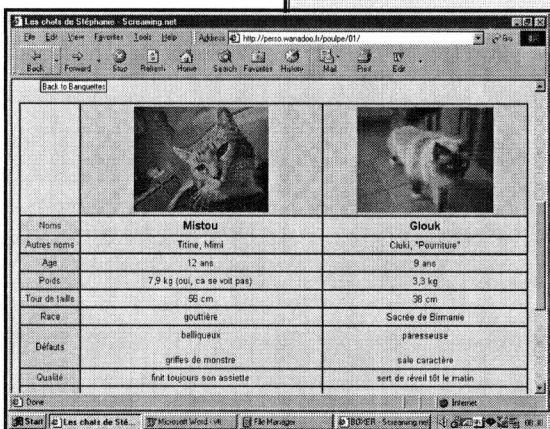

Pupils gather information from websites to support work on food, leisure and animals

INFOTECH

Putting achievement first

Ensuring appropriate training

Teachers need to be trained to plan the use of ICT to support learning, to use ICT effectively in their teaching and to evaluate pupils' progress as a result of using ICT.

The development plan will therefore need to identify:

- what training is necessary, e.g.
  training in the use of a specific programme or application, observing another teacher working with a class, curriculum planning;

- when and where this training will take place, e.g.
  in school, at home, at an outside location, on line;

- who will provide the training, e.g.
  a member of the department, a member of the school's ICT team, an external trainer, a training document/manual.

Ensuring that pupils have the necessary knowledge, skills and understanding (MFL) for the planned work, e.g.

they must know how to:

- draft and redraft, in order to use a word processor effectively;
- skim and scan text in order to select appropriate material from the Internet.

Finding out if pupils have the necessary knowledge, skills and understanding (ICT) for the planned work, e.g.

have they already learnt elsewhere in the curriculum how to carry out complex searches in order to carry out a planned MFL data handling task?

Ensuring that staff are competent to teach new ICT skills if they are required, e.g.

using an Internet search engine, copying a graph from a data handling package into a word processor.

Management

Identifying necessary tasks within the development plan and ensuring that they are completed requires management qualities that:

31

INFO TECH

Putting achievement first

- promote efficiency;
- make good use of time;
- deploy resources (both human and physical) effectively;

all of which contribute to good working relationships and the raising of staff morale.

The departmental ICT policy

An effective ICT policy (see chapter 3) will make it easier to carry out this type of planning because it will contain:

- a clear rationale for the use of ICT;
- a description of current use of ICT in the department;
- details of available resources;
- details of staff competence and experience;
- information about staff development opportunities;
- information about roles, responsibilities and channels of communication.

32

The departmental profile

The detail and emphasis of development planning is likely to be affected by the levels of awareness, experience and competence within the department. For example, if staff need to be convinced that ICT is not merely a whim or a fad:

- emphasis will need to be given to describing outcomes and, if possible, providing evidence from pilot work;
- required use of ICT will need to be simple, easy to manage and well supported;
- training will need to be thorough and appropriate;
- planned classroom support may be necessary.

If, however, teachers are technically competent, already have positive experience of ICT use with pupils, and are aware of the power and potential of ICT to raise achievement:

- teaching strategies may be further refined;
- new initiatives with individual teachers may be encouraged;
- opportunities for developing pupils' ICT capability may be identified.

Planned classroom support may be necessary

THE SCHEME OF WORK

Purpose

The purpose of the departmental scheme of work is to provide explicit support and guidance concerning teaching, so that there is consistent provision between classes and consistent progress across a key stage.

33

An effective scheme of work will therefore play a key role in raising standards and securing equality of access to the curriculum for all pupils.

The use of ICT by pupils must be integrated into the scheme of work if entitlement is to be achieved. In deciding on where and how to deploy software designed specifically for use in MFL, a full evaluation is necessary. A software evaluation form is included as an appendix. (p59)

ICT in the scheme of work

The use of ICT can be recorded in the scheme of work at one of three levels:

Minimum level

At this level ICT use is briefly recorded in the form of opportunities linked to units of work, e.g.

pupils could use a word processor to write an account of a holiday

rather than **requirements.**

This approach may help raise awareness and may stimulate some teachers to use ICT with their classes. However, it is unlikely to ensure entitlement, promote

INFOTECH

Putting achievement first

consistency or raise standards across a whole year group, even if teachers are technically competent and access to resources is guaranteed. This is because:

- there is no guarantee that all teachers will take up the suggested opportunities;
- there is no mention of the 'appropriate / value-added' dimension of ICT use, in terms of language to be learnt or knowledge to be demonstrated.

Medium level

At this level ICT use is recorded in the form of a **requirement** which has been planned for by ensuring access to resources and appropriate staff training. The descriptions are a little more detailed than for the minimum level, e.g.

with text books and exercise books as reference materials, pupils use a word processor to draft and redraft an account (real or imagined) of what they did on their last birthday: the work will include time spent in the classroom on learning and practising the skills of drafting and redrafting.

34

This approach sets out to meet entitlement. It also shows the need for work both at and away from the computer. However, because there is not a clear picture of:

- content (in terms of length, range of vocabulary, points of language);

or

- process (how the drafting and redrafting should be organised and/or taught);

there is still a risk of inconsistent outcomes from pupil to pupil and from class to class.

Maximum level

At this level ICT use, along with preparation and follow-up, is recorded in considerable detail. The description below is very full, including almost everything conceivable that could be included to guarantee entitlement, consistency and achievement.

● Activity

Using their text books and exercise books as reference materials, pupils word-process an account (real or imagined) of what they did on their last birthday.

● Learning intentions

Pupils produce a written account (approx. 100 words) of a past event using:
– perfect and imperfect tenses;
– 1st person singular and plural verb forms;
– time references;
– opinions.
and improve the account (in terms of accuracy and quality) through redrafting.

● Reason for using ICT

Word processing is the most efficient means of enabling pupils to redraft work for improved accuracy, range of language and presentation.

● Previous knowledge – MFL

Pupils will need to know how to use the perfect tense to describe events in the past.

They must also have practised using 'j'étais' and 'c'était', with adjectives, to express feelings and opinions.

● Previous knowledge – ICT

35

All pupils will have acquired basic word processing skills in other curriculum areas. However, they will need to be taught how to create accented characters.

Use the ALT key and a number. Hold down the ALT key, type the relevant number *on the numeric keypad and not on the top line of the keyboard.* Release the ALT key.

FRENCH		GERMAN		SPANISH		ITALIAN		NORDIC	
à	133	ä	132	á	160	à	133	å	134
â	131	Ä	142	é	130	è	138	Å	143
ç	135	ö	148	í	161	É	144	æ	145
Ç	128	Ö	153	ñ	164	ì	141	Æ	146
é	130	ü	129	Ñ	165	ò	149	ä	132
è	138	Ü	154	ó	162	ù	151	Ä	142
ê	136	ß	225	ú	163			ö	148
ë	137			¿	168			Ö	153
î	140			¡	173			ø	236
ï	139							Ø	237
ô	147								
ù	151								
û	150								

Pupils will need to be taught how to create accented characters

● Process

Give pupils a clear picture of the sort of language that could be used in their descriptions, e.g.

– the perfect tense to describe what happened (e.g. j'ai fait une boum*);*
– use of nous *as well as* je*;*
– time references (e.g. à trois heures, ensuite*);*
– opinions (e.g. c'était intéressant et amusant*).*

Get pupils to draft their accounts using a common font and font size (i.e. presentation is not an issue). Make sure they know that they will have the opportunity to redraft at a later stage.

Get printouts of the first drafts and mark them by identifying up to six simple errors in each piece of work (e.g. la zoo, j'invité, ammusant*) with a highlighter pen.*

Return the work and ask pupils to look at their own errors. Get two or three pupils to explain and rectify an error in front of the class. Pupils then work in pairs, attempting to explain their errors to each other.

Next, help pupils, by way of example and discussion, to think about how they might improve the quality of their writing, e.g.

– linking two simple sentences;
– by extending the range of vocabulary.

Pupils now redraft their work.

● Outcomes

Show the class numerous examples of how pupils have made their work more accurate and more interesting.

Get pupils to reflect upon their use of ICT in the context of drafting and redrafting. The ensuing discussion could include the following observations, which will support further appropriate use of a word processor:

– Using a word processor gives confidence in the first draft, because you know that it can be corrected and improved later. This leads to more adventurous work.

– Redrafting is quick and easy. You can focus on the errors and correct them efficiently. You do not have to waste time recopying the whole passage. The work looks good.

– You can easily improve your work by adding new words and phrases.

36

INFO TECH

Putting achievement first

● Programme of Study references – MFL

Pupils should be taught how to:

– *express themselves using a range of vocabulary and structures;*
– *develop their independence in learning and using the target language;*
– *express and discuss personal feelings and opinions;*
– *redraft their writing to improve its accuracy and presentation.*

● Programme of Study references – ICT (Key Stage 3)

Pupils should be taught to:

– *use a range of ICT tools efficiently to draft, bring together and refine information;*
– *reflect critically on their own and others' use of ICT to help them develop and improve their ideas and the quality of their work.*

A sense of proportion

37

Don't worry if your scheme does not look like this. Remember:

- Rome was not built in a day. An effective scheme of work is a working tool, used by teachers and constantly evolving. It is a means to an end, not a work of art.

- Schemes of work may be beautifully written, but are not always used in practice, and much can be achieved on the basis of ongoing discussion and experience.

- Some descriptions could be very detailed (e.g. when entitlement is required); others could be simpler (e.g. when ICT use is optional).

OTHER ASPECTS OF PLANNING

Planning for differentiation

The principles established in this book concerning appropriate use of ICT and effective planning must apply to all pupils, irrespective of their age or ability.

Managers observing these principles can best plan for differentiation, not by producing unmanageable quantities of differentiated tasks and materials, but by reflecting on the possibilities for:

Differentiation within a program, e.g.
when a text manipulation program provides different ways of rebuilding a text, as well as different ways in which pupils can get help.

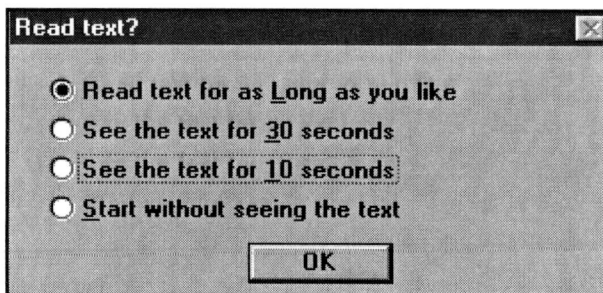

Read text? ☒

⦿ Read text for as Long as you like

◯ See the text for 30 seconds

◯ See the text for 10 seconds

◯ Start without seeing the text

[OK]

Text manipulation programs provide different ways in which pupils can get help

38

Differentiation by outcome, e.g.
when pupils search for information on the Internet; when they carry out a creative writing task.

Differentiation by choice, e.g.
when pupils choose from a range of pre-selected texts available on a school's intranet system: when they choose what software to use to produce a presentation; when they choose whether or not to use ICT to carry out a task.

Differentiation by time
Always possible, because the computer is infinitely patient, allowing individuals to take as long as they need before making the next move. This can lead to · problems, however, when work has to be fitted into lessons of a fixed duration.

Planning for pupils with special needs

ICT is an appropriate tool for pupils with special needs. Key features of ICT that support motivation and achievement for all, e.g.
control of the pace of work, speed of computer response, depth and quantity of information, ease of access to information, ease with which mistakes can be corrected, ability to present work well, opportunities for problem solving and risk taking
have been proved to have particular impact on pupils with learning, behavioural and emotional difficulties.

Info Tech
Putting achievement first

Specific ICT applications (e.g. multimedia), programs (e.g. a dedicated CD-ROM) and devices (e.g. a speech synthesiser) may be essential for providing access to the curriculum for children with profound and multiple learning difficulties. When this is the case, they should be used.

Much pilot work and research have gone into the use of ICT for pupils with special needs and are well documented by organisations such as CILT and BECTA.

Planning for use of the target language

The following observations may help leaders and managers wishing to .maximise both teacher and pupil use of the target language when using ICT.

(i) Use of the target language with ICT will reflect its use in the department as a whole, i.e. an effective TL policy, consistently applied, will provide a secure foundation for use in an ICT context.

(ii) Whichever approaches and conventions are used, pupils are helped by consistency within and across classes.

(iii) There may be times when the teacher feels that English needs to be used for a specific purpose, e.g. explaining a point of structure, teaching a new procedure or technique.

(iv) Managers and teachers will need to reach agreement over:

– essential ICT vocabulary to be used in the target language, e.g. print, save, screen, mouse, click on...

– specialist vocabulary related to a particular task, application or piece of software, e.g. 'call up the browser', 'make a graph';

– prior knowledge to be reinforced, e.g. the alphabet, 'your turn', 'that's right', 'well done!'

(v) Teachers will also need to decide whether to attempt to use target language terms (e.g. file, open, view, format) if these are normally displayed on screen in English.

(vi) Use of the target language is easier with closed tasks, e.g. using the 'prediction' option in a text manipulation program. It is more difficult with open tasks, e.g. making presentations. It is extremely difficult (and is

39

INFOTECH
Putting achievement first

therefore not to be recommended) when asking Key Stage 3 pupils to reflect in depth on their use of ICT, e.g. was it effective, appropriate?

(vii) Teachers using predominantly the target language and pupils using predominantly the mother tongue may be acceptable and appropriate at certain times and in certain contexts. However, good management will find ways of helping all pupils to progress. At the very least, it must ensure that the quality and quantity of target language use with/by older pupils using ICT is greater than that of their younger counterparts.

N.B. Sheets listing target language ICT terminology in a wide range of languages are available from BECTA.

CONCLUSIONS

40

Effective planning is a key factor to achieving consistency, high standards and meeting pupil entitlement since it will:

- ensure that progress takes place – and is maintained;
- help minimise the impact of adversity (e.g. the departure of a key teacher);
- help maximise the impact of an opportunity (e.g. the availability of new resources, the implementation of a national training programme);
- enable the department to meet National Curriculum and inspection requirements;
- give the department control of an essential tool for raising achievement.

It will also provide a basis for effective monitoring and evaluation in terms of the quality of teaching and learning. These will be dealt with in the next chapter.

INFOTECH
Putting achievement first

5 Monitoring for achievement

This chapter assumes that:

- no matter how well a department plans its work, quality of teaching is probably the most important factor influencing pupil attainment;
- unlike many factors (pupils' socio-economic background, etc), teaching quality is something that schools can control;
- some aspects of teaching contribute towards attainment more than others.

It must also be noted, however, that the monitoring of teaching and learning is a weakness in some MFL departments. The OFSTED publication '*Standards in the secondary curriculum 1997/8*' states:

Some departments monitor practice and progress very carefully; others have scarcely addressed the issues. The more successful usually have a structured approach to monitoring of pupils' work (for example, heads of department sampling exercise books) and of teaching (observation of lessons by colleagues).

It will therefore be necessary to set out some ideas for:

- key features of effective MFL teaching to be used in monitoring;
- approaches to monitoring teaching and learning;
- using the evidence that has been collected.

KEY FEATURES OF EFFECTIVE MFL TEACHING

Four key features of effective MFL teaching, namely:

(i) setting clear learning intentions;
(ii) distinguishing between different types of language;

(iii) modelling;

(iv) checking for learning;

are suggested as criteria for monitoring MFL lessons, including lessons involving ICT.

They have emerged from recent work in which the author has been involved at both local and national levels. This work has included lesson observations, as well as discussions with advisers, inspectors, head teachers, teachers and pupils.

These features may seem obvious, unremarkable and unglamorous. Nevertheless, it is true that, consistently applied over time, they have a proven impact on attainment.

They are more appropriate and easier to use in monitoring than:

- criteria based on personal styles, e.g. teacher shows a sense of humour and gives lots of praise (which may be inappropriate);

42

- criteria that are not directly and unambiguously related to attainment, e.g. pupils are very active (but may not all be learning); teacher gives help to individuals (possibly because work was not clearly explained in the first place).

The above features should be seen as relevant to pupils of all ages and abilities, and to all lessons, irrespective of the way the classroom is organised (carousel of activities with one or more ICT-based, one computer supporting a whole-class activity, whole class in computer room, pupils working in LRC, etc).

Description and exemplification in an ICT context

The four key features of effective teaching will now be described and then exemplified in the context of a Year 7 French class which has been following a unit of the text book in which they learn to give simple opinions about items of food and drink. They are then expected to combine their new learning (opinions) with previously learnt vocabulary (school subjects, colours, etc). To support this they are required to work in pairs in a computer room, using the following text that has been written by a member of the department and then saved into a text manipulation program:

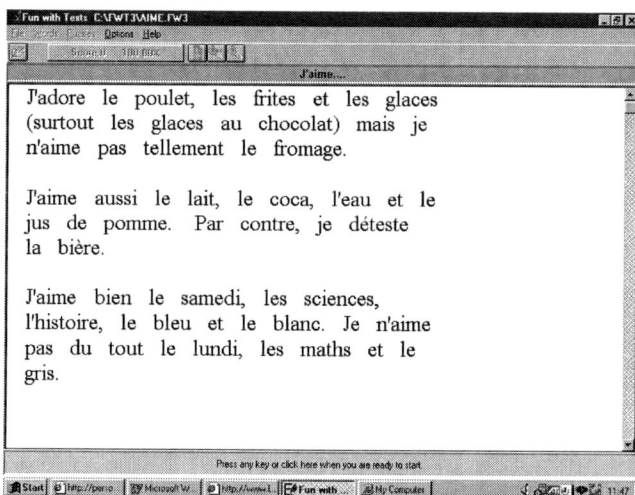

Following this activity, they will be expected to produce their own piece of writing which should be of a similar length and standard.

43

Setting learning intentions

This involves the teacher having a precise picture of the language, techniques or concepts to be learnt and then demonstrated during a lesson or series of lessons.

In the given context, these are the learning intentions set by the teacher:

By the end of the unit of work all pupils will be able to write approx. 50 words about things they like and dislike. Their writing will include at least:

- two different expressions of liking;
- two different expressions of disliking;
- two items of food and two items of drink;
- one new item of food or drink, found in a dictionary and prefixed by the correct definite article;
- one item from a previously covered topic area (e.g. days of the week, colours, school subjects);
- three of the following words/expressions: *et, mais, surtout, par contre.*

It should be apparent from this that:

- the text manipulation program is not simply to be used as an enjoyable

INFO TECH

Putting achievement first

activity. It leads on from previous work in the classroom (e.g. learning the necessary vocabulary, asking and answering questions) and is linked to a planned outcome (the pupil writing);

- the learning intentions are detailed. They are not vague and imprecise, e.g. 'pupils will write about things they like and dislike'. This precision will require the teaching to have structure and purpose.

Distinguishing between different types of language

Observation and research have shown that pupils, when working with a 'topic-based' syllabus, need explicit guidance if they are to distinguish readily between:

- vocabulary (e.g. *vin, samedi*) linked closely to the topic unit;

and

- essential language items (e.g. the definite article in *j'aime le poulet,* the words *et, mais, surtout, par contre*) that can help them produce sentences of their own, move beyond the 'chunk' and the topic and become more independent and confident users of the language.

44

It will therefore be crucial for the Year 7 teacher to ensure that pupils understand the higher 'currency value' of these essential items, not just in the context of the immediate task, but also as an 'investment' in future progress. This will need to be done in lessons preceding the text manipulation activity, during the activity itself, and in the follow-up lesson when the written task is set.

Modelling

Modelling is closely linked to setting clear learning intentions. It involves:

- giving pupils a clear picture of what constitutes a good response to a task – so they do not have to second-guess what the teacher expects from them; and then
- showing them how to produce the response themselves by emulating the model.

Text manipulation programs such as *Fun With Texts* provide a powerful and unique vehicle for the production and presentation of written models that pupils can explore, practise and internalise.

Few pupils, however, will be able to go on to emulate such models without specific guidance from the teacher (e.g. how to use a dictionary appropriately, how to apply the definite article to a new item of vocabulary, how to link two simple sentences with *mais*).

Checking for learning

This could take the form of:

- On-the-spot checks carried out during the lesson to make sure that **all** pupils have grasped a point or can do a specific thing. Techniques for doing this include:
  - whole class response (hands up; class told explicitly that absence of a response means they have a problem);
  - teacher samples by checking with individuals – not always the reliable few who are guaranteed to get the point!

as well as

- 'Fixing', i.e. re-stating and recapping the key learning points at the end of the lesson/unit. Techniques for doing this include:
  - summarising what has been achieved;
  - asking pupils to explain in as much detail as possible what they have **learnt** (rather than what they have **done**);
  - asking pupils to give examples of a new pattern/point of language.

45

In the context of the text manipulation activity, on-the-spot checks are made by the program itself – when it responds to the pupils' input.

They could also be made by the teacher observing individuals and discussing their work.

Checks could include pupils reflecting on how/why using a text manipulation program can help their learning.

More examples

Here are two further examples of how these key features of effective teaching should also be evident in ICT contexts.

Example 1

Context

Low-ability pupils needing vocabulary reinforcement work individually with a multimedia CD-ROM to practise listening and responding.

Setting learning intentions

The teacher has a clear idea of the vocabulary to be acquired, as well as the number of practice activities pupils should be able to complete over a period of 30 minutes.

The pupils know what is expected of them.

Modelling

The program itself, when operating in 'example' mode, provides models of how pupils should respond. The teacher checks that this has been understood.

Checking for learning

As the teacher observes the pupils she must decide if, when and how to intervene:

a) if a pupil appears to have difficulties;
b) to get individual feedback on what is being learnt;
c) to remind the group as a whole of the targets that have been set.

Time is set aside at the end of the lesson to fix what has been learnt. This includes discussing whether, and if so why, the use of ICT has been helpful.

46

Example 2

Context

Pupils seek information from a datafile about favourite subjects, sports and pastimes of German children. They report back findings orally for partners to note down.

Setting learning intentions

The teacher is clear about the reading skills that he expects pupils to demonstrate when interrogating the datafile. He also expects his pupils to speak to their partners in full sentences when transferring the information

Modelling

Prior to the activity taking place, the teacher gives a lesson in which he uses a single record from the datafile (displayed on the OHP) as a basis for modelling the skills and techniques he wishes his pupils to demonstrate (e.g. how to deduce meaning using context and cognates; how to develop sentences incorporating the words and short phrases displayed; the note-taking part of the activity; how to ask a partner to repeat/speak more clearly/spell a word).

He then provides another record from the datafile to give the pupils opportunities to practise what they have been taught.

At the beginning of the ICT activity, the process of interrogating the datafile is initially modelled by the teacher.

Distinguishing between different types of language

To prepare for the activity, the teacher emphasises the essential points of language (e.g. 3rd person use of the verb, use of possessive pronouns, use of negatives) that pupils will need to know and apply when building sentences.

Checking for learning

Having given time for pupils to practise during the preparation stage, the teacher samples the responses of a small number of pupils. A key point is reinforced when it becomes evident that difficulties are still being experienced.

During the ICT activity, the teacher carefully monitors the quality of the language used. If necessary, he intervenes in order to bring about improvement in pronunciation or sentence structure.

At the end of the activity, time is set aside for pupils to explain and discuss what they have demonstrated in terms of new vocabulary, ability to manipulate language, etc. They also comment on whether the data-handling activity was a useful and appropriate vehicle for the task, e.g. did it help them respond to the unexpected? did it make them work hard? did it simulate a situation that they might be expected to deal with in real life?

MONITORING TEACHING

Having established some criteria for effective teaching, it is now necessary to look at ways in which monitoring might occur. Of course, individual schools and departments may already have agreed procedures of their own, but if this is not the case, the following two approaches could be considered:

Data collection

This method provides a checklist of key features that could be identified in a single lesson or over a series of lessons in which the use of ICT is included.

It expands on the agreed criteria.

Used with a range of teachers and over a range of lessons it could provide information to inform a departmental action plan.

Items to be included in a checklist could be as follows:

48

Lesson observation: data collection sheet

Learning intentions

Teacher is clear about what is to be learnt	
Pupils are clear about what they are to learn	
Learning intentions are challenging	
Learning intentions are achievable	
Learning intentions build on previous knowledge (MFL)	
Learning intentions build on previous knowledge (ICT)	
Activities support the learning intentions	
Activities are presented in an appropriate sequence	
Pupils are clear about how to carry out the activities	
Pupils understand the purpose of the activities	

Different types of language

Teacher demonstrates/emphasises different levels of language ☐

Pupils understand these differences ☐

Pupils can apply their understanding ☐

Modelling

Teacher gives pupils a clear model of what constitutes a good response ☐

Pupils are taught how to emulate the model ☐

49

Checking for learning

During the lesson steps are taken to ensure that all pupils are learning ☐

Adjustments are made within the lesson if problems emerge ☐

Steps are taken to find out whether all pupils have mastered the key points ☐

✓	Seen to a significant extent
✗	Seen to a limited extent
	Not seen at all
NA	Not appropriate

Recording judgements

This method, which involves the observer taking notes and making judgements during a single lesson, is a more intensive way of gathering evidence.

INFO TECH

Putting achievement first

It could be most useful when leading to informed discussion with individual teachers.

Judgements should broadly relate to the agreed criteria and could look something like this:

- 'The learning intentions were clear and they related to the scheme of work.'
- 'Pupils were clear about the standard of work required, but some were not sure about how to achieve it.'
- 'Good use was made by pupils of grammatical terminology and ICT terminology.'
- 'Poor pronunciation was allowed to go unchallenged.'
- 'Most pupils offered responses when fixing took place, but a few remained passive.'
- 'Not enough time was set aside for fixing. The end of the lesson was rushed.'

Additional observations, e.g.

- 'Pupils clearly enjoyed their work.'
- 'Nearly all pupils remained on task.'

could also be useful.

MONITORING THE 'VALUE-ADDED' IN LEARNING

Finding out whether pupils are learning has already been explored, to some extent, in the guidance on monitoring teaching. In this guidance evidence of learning is seen to emerge as a result of good teaching in contexts where ICT has played a part in achieving a planned outcome.

However, there is an additional dimension to monitoring learning – that of looking uniquely for the exclusive 'value-added' contribution that ICT claims to make, and without which there is little point in the investment of teachers' time, expertise and resources.

Sadly little or no formal research has been done to investigate either the motivational or the learning potential of computers in the MFL classroom. Teachers

50

may feel that motivation and learning improve through using ICT but, as Professor Graham Davies pointed out in a message on the Lingu@net Forum (28/5/99):

'We don't know how long motivation lasts. Likewise, none of us can be sure that presentation of an item involving several perceptual channels (as in a multimedia presentation) helps students learn better than when they are presented with an item in one perceptual mode only.'

With this in mind, whilst we await relevant and overdue research findings, teachers should continue to look for 'value-added' gains in learning, but in the short term only. Some areas to investigate are listed below.

When using ICT

- increased perseverance; pupils stay on task and want to keep working at the end of the lesson;
- a high level of pupil-pupil interaction (relating to language, rather than how to use the software) when working in pairs;
- pupils seeing how language works;
- pupils working and thinking independently;
- pupils prepared to take risks;
- needs of individual pupils being met;
- pupils showing obvious signs of enjoyment, as a result of having met a challenge.

After using ICT

- an improved standard of work (e.g. the length and accuracy of a piece of writing, the range of language and vocabulary used in an oral presentation, improved reading skills, better pronunciation) achieved by the majority – in comparison with work produced by pupils of similar ability in previous years;
- more pupils showing awareness of how language works;
- increased knowledge of and interest in other countries and cultures;
- pupils showing understanding of why a particular activity using ICT was helpful.

51

INFO TECH

Putting achievement first

USING THE EVIDENCE

Findings arising from monitoring procedures should be discussed in departmental meeting time. Too many departmental meetings are taken up with routine administration that could be dealt with in other ways.

Some findings can be shared and points of action can be agreed, recorded and easily implemented, e.g.

- *teachers x and y (who are not confident in the use of an Internet search engine) to arrange a short session with teacher z (who is);*

- *everyone to make more time for discussing with pupils the value of ICT in their learning – and report back at the next meeting.*

Others may require a more systematic response at the level of the departmental development plan, e.g.

52

- *there is a clear need to develop a more structured approach for teaching the skills of drafting and redrafting to all pupils – in order to help them make better use of the word processor's potential to support these skills.*

Others may need to be followed-up on an individual basis, e.g.

- *there is non-compliance or poor performance: if this occurs, criticism must be based on evidence, advice must be given on how to improve – and an agreed date must be fixed for the next observation: negative feedback should not be given publicly.*

POINTS TO CONSIDER

It is the Head of Department's responsibility to ensure that monitoring takes place.

Some monitoring tasks can be delegated to individuals, e.g. interviewing pupils, observing the lesson of a competent and experienced colleague. Others, requiring a judgmental stance or involving line management, should only be undertaken by the Head of Department. There are also tasks that could be undertaken by the whole department, e.g. scrutinising written work.

Monitoring should be seen as a routine process, not a special event.

Observations should not be unannounced.

Senior management must take active steps to enable monitoring to take place. They also have the right to share findings.

Monitoring is an important tool for achieving consistency, so that whichever teacher takes the class should make minimal difference to how the subject is taught and how well the pupils achieve.

¡HOLA!

53

Observations should not be unannounced

INFOTECH
Putting achievement first

6 Sharing information

AN E-MAIL DISCUSSION GROUP

This book has set out to give practical guidance that will be relevant and useful to all MFL departments.

It can also help individuals to exchange ideas, ask questions and share success (whilst at the same time using ICT effectively!) by directing them to the **Lingu@NET forum.**

What is the Lingu@NET forum?

The Lingu@NET forum is an e-mail discussion group for all those involved in language teaching and research. It is available free of charge to anyone with an e-mail address. If you can send and receive e-mail, you can take part in the Lingu@NET forum.

How do I join?

Detailed joining instructions are provided on the Lingu@NET forum website at:

www.mailbase.ac.uk/
lists/linguanet-forum

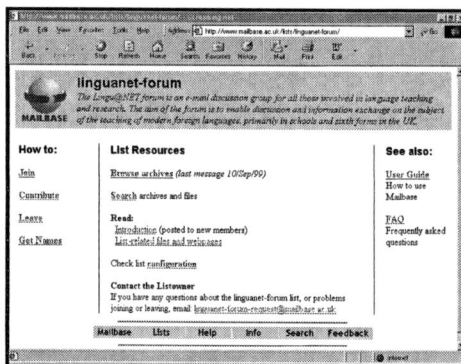

What sort of issues concerning ICT management could I raise?

Anything and everything. Managing ICT for pupil achievement is no easy task. Don't kid yourself that everyone else is doing it better than you. So feel free to air any concern, e.g.

I need to know whether all pupils in Year 8 are able to make presentations combining text and pictures, but nobody in the school seems able to give me an answer. How should I deal with this problem in the long and short term?

I want to book time in one of the school's computer rooms, but I have been told that history and science have priority. Is this fair and what should I do? P.S. The school does not have a cross-curricular ICT steering group.

I want my pupils to use data handling in their MFL work. Should I look for a data handling package that is easy to use (possibly with menus in French) or should I try to get to grips with the package (which looks very complicated) that is used elsewhere in the school?

What do you do as a head of department when a colleague just cannot seem to get to grips with ICT at all, despite support being provided?

55

I want to start using ICT across the whole department with at least one application. Where should I begin? Text manipulation? Word processing? Using the Internet? Which year should I target?

You might also wish to tell others about your successes, e.g.

I made arrangements to work for half of a whole-school INSET day with our ICT co-ordinator. It has really helped us because she is now far more aware of our needs and is working with us to provide a flexible training programme and increased access to resources.

Over the past year the department has been using text manipulation and word processing to help Year 8 pupils explore and emulate models of pupil writing based on performance at level 4 in AT4. The result... an increase of 50% in pupils achieving this level by the end of Year 8. Fantastic! Next stop – models of Grade A writing for pupils in Years 10 and 11!

I have been asking Year 11 pupils to compare the language of e-mail messages with that of a formal letter. Their findings were very perceptive, e.g.

■ *there is no need to write the date and time, because this is done automatically;*

Sharing information

- greetings are informal; the tone is one of a conversation rather than a letter;
- short phrases are frequently used instead of extended sentences;
- abbreviations (mn, tél) are acceptable.

They then applied their understanding by composing an e-mail message of their own and sending it to a hotel in France, requesting information about prices and facilities. Very motivating, especially when there was a rapid answer.

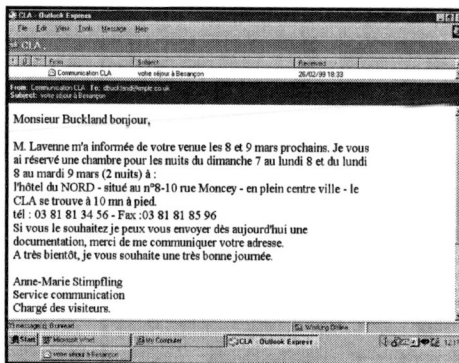

56

Just found an excellent website to support teaching the weather. It will predict the next five days' weather for a range of French towns. Good visuals, uncomplicated, simple vocabulary. I have used it with Year 7 classes to reinforce vocabulary and with Year 10 classes to practise the future tense. Find it on: http://fr.weather.yahoo.com/Europe/france

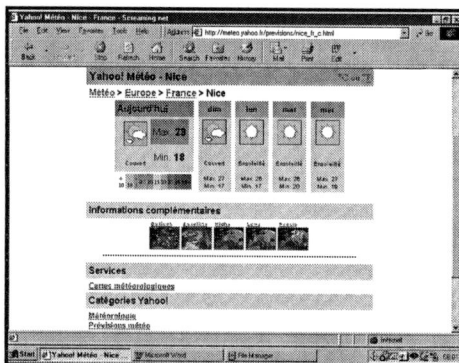

INFOTECH
Putting achievement first

7 | Final thoughts

To conclude, here are ten key issues relating to the role and status of ICT in schools that may get you thinking about where you are now and what the future holds.

1. ICT just taught as a discrete subject will not take pupils forward.

2. Further hard evidence is needed of the impact that ICT can make on learning in each curriculum area.

3. Teachers using ICT can improve their understanding of how pupils learn.

4. The pedagogies and methodologies of teaching with ICT need to be researched and disseminated.

5. This evidence should inform directly ICT teacher training, in order to raise standards further in this area.

6. To make real progress with ICT, teachers must have access to their own computer at home.

7. Teachers alone cannot be expected to manage increasing amount of ICT in schools. A career structure must be developed for resource managers to work in schools assisting teachers.

8. Computers in pupils' homes are a growing and vastly under-used resource. Schools need to address this within the contexts of

   a) raising achievement;
   b) ensuring equal opportunities.

INFOTECH
Putting achievement first

9. The recent commitment of the DfEE, Welsh Office, SOEED and the Northern Ireland Libraries Board to the development of ICT in schools must be maintained.

10. Funding through education-business partnerships needs to increase.

58

8 Appendix

EVALUATING SOFTWARE

Learner independence

What level of guidance/prior knowledge (MFL) will the learner need in order to work independently?

What level of guidance/prior knowledge (ICT) will the learner need in order to work independently?

Will this work be interesting / appropriate / challenging?

Learning objectives

What current learning objectives will it help you meet?

Can it change the way in which current objectives are met?

Can it alter / refine / extend your learning objectives?

Content

What does the software provide in terms of:

- language content and range?

- opportunities for improvement/achievement in each of the attainment targets?

- opportunities to deliver parts of the National Curriculum programme of study, e.g.
  - the principles and interrelationship of sounds and writing in the target language;

  - the grammar of the target language;

  - listening, reading or viewing for personal interest and enjoyment;

  - responding to different types of spoken and written language

  - working with authentic materials;

  - redrafting writing to improve its accuracy and presentation;

  - skimming and scanning written texts for information.

Structure/design

How easy is it to operate?

Is the design clear?

Are the instructions / prompts / links easy to understand?

Why bother?

What (if anything) makes it different/better?

60

INFO TECH

Putting achievement first

9 References

PUBLICATIONS

Atkinson T, *Info Tech3 – WWW/The Internet* (CILT 1998)

Atkinson T, *Hands off! It's my go! IT in the languages classroom* (CILT and NCET, 1992)

Brown J, Howlett F, *IT works* (NCET, 1994)

Hewer S, *Info Tech 2 – Text manipulation: computer-based activities to improve knowledge and use of the target language* (CILT 1997)

Kenny J, *ICT in schools: a new reality* (Xemplar Education, 1998)

Lee J, *CILT Briefing 2 – writing schemes of work* (CILT, 2000)

Lee J, Buckland D, Shaw G, *The Invisible Child* (CILT, 1998)

Rowe S, *Managing subject departments for pupil achievement* (Folens, 1998)

Townshend K, *Info Tech 1 – E-mail: using electronic communication in foreign language teaching* (CILT 1997)

Accent on IT: an MFL/IT INSET pack for Key Stage 3 (NCET, 1997)

Approaches to IT Capability: Key Stage 3 (MFL) (NCET, 1995)

Information Technology in the National Curriculum: consultation document (QCA, 1999)

IT across the curriculum: a way forward (Herts IT, 1991)

MFL/ICT information sheets (CILT/BECTA)

61

INFO TECH
Putting achievement first

MFL – an entitlement to IT (NCET, 1996)

Modern Foreign Languages in the National Curriculum: consultation document (QCA, 1999)

National standards for subject leaders (Teacher Training Agency, 1998)

Standards in the secondary curriculum 1997/8 (OFSTED, 1999)

Using ICT to meet teaching objectives in MFL: identification of training needs (Teacher Training Agency, 1999)

Whole school IT development (University of Sussex, Brighton Polytechnic, 1991)

WEBSITES

CILT
www.cilt.org.uk

Leicestershire Comenius Centre
www.leics-comenius.org.uk

Yahoo! France
fr.yahoo.com   de.yahoo.com   es.yahoo.com

Camsoft
www.camsoftpartners.co.uk

Lingu@NET
www.linguanet.org.uk

MFLIT – the MFL section of the National Grid for Learning's 'Virtual Teacher Centre'
vtc.ngfl.gov.uk/resource/cits/mfl

Lingu@NET Forum
www.mailbase.ac.uk/lists/linguanet-forum

ICT4LT
www.ict4lt.org

National Grid for Learning
www.ngfl.gov.uk/ngfl/index.html

INFOTECH

Putting achievement first

Virtual Teachers' Centre
vtc.ngfl.gov.uk

ADDRESSES

Association for Language Learning
150 Railway Terrace
Rugby CV21 3HN
Tel: 01788 546443
Fax: 01788 544149

Camsoft (software publishers)
10 Wheatfield Close, Maidenhead, Berks SL63PS
Tel and fax: 01628 825 206
E-mail: GrahamDavies1@compuserve.com

BECTA (British Educational Communications and Technology Agency – formerly NCET)
Milburn Hill Road, Science Park, Coventry CV4 7JJ
Tel: 01203 416 994
Fax: 01203 411418
E-mail: Becta@becta.org.uk

Leicestershire Comenius Centre
Quorn Hall
Meynell Road
Loughborough LE12 8BG
Tel: 01509 416990
Fax: 01509 416993
E-mail: pam@leics-comenius.org.uk

63

INFO TECH
Putting achievement first

References

National Association of Advisers for Computers in Education (NAACE)
PO Box 60
Tipton
West Midlands DY4 0YS
Tel: 0121 530 9732
Fax: 0121 530 9732
E-mail: mikesmith@rmplc.co.uk
www.naace.org

National Association of Language Advisers (NALA)
17 West Avenue
Gosforth
Newcastle-upon-Tyne
NE3 4ES
Tel: 0191 284 2919

64

TEXT MANIPULATION SOFTWARE

Fun with Texts
published and distributed by Camsoft

Using communications technology in language learning

INFO TeCH

Series Editor: Sue Hewer

5

The **InfoTech** series helps modern language teachers to keep their practice up to date in the rapidly changing world of learning technology and communications media. In the style of the popular CILT **Pathfinder** series, each book presents well-tried strategies for using computers and on-line media to promote effective language learning, to bring the target language into the classroom, and to provide learners with real communication opportunities

If ICT is to support learning and raise pupils' achievement in modern foreign languages, then teachers and heads of department need to understand how it can be integrated successfully into the departmental languages programme. This book demonstrates the importance of effective management and shows how to do it in an ordinary school in the 'real' world. Step-by-step guidance on how to start, how to plan and implement, and how to sustain the planning process at all times is exemplified by case studies. **Putting achievement first** is a must for teachers, HoDs, IT co-ordinators and school managers.

David Buckland *is an advisory teacher for MFL in the London Borough of Barking and Dagenham, previously Head of Department and Senior Teacher in a Hertfordshire comprehensive school. He has written ICT materials to support published MFL courses and has experience in website design. He has also worked with the DfEE in producing materials and guidance to support the use of ICT in the National Curriculum.*

ISBN 1-902031-63-6

9 781902 031637

CiLT
Centre for Information
on Language Teaching and Research

www.cilt.org.uk